BRAVING THE BIG FREEZE

by Madeline Tyler &
Sam Thompson

Minneapolis, Minnesota

Credits

Images are courtesy of Shutterstock.com. With thanks to Getty Images, Thinkstock Photo, and iStockphoto. Recurring images – mycteria, benchart, Andrii_Malysh, Bohdan Populov, Anastasiia Veretennikova, Francois Poirier. Cover – Zerbor, jakkapan, nayuki minase. 4–5 – Esteban De Armas, FedBul. 6–7 – Aunt Spray, Rashevskyi Viacheslav, Yaroslav Vitkovskiy. 8–9 – Bluemoon 1981, Lisina Margarita, Mathias Berlin. 10–11 – Africa Studio, Ibrahim Buraganov, Sambulov Yevgeniy. 12–13 – Maximillian cabinet, PrimeMockup, Salienko Evgenii, Volodymyr Baleha. 14–15 – ChiccoDodiFC, FabrikaSimf, mady70, Vereshchagin Dmitry. 16–17 – Bianca Grueneberg, Picture Partners, solarseven, Valery Evlakhov. 18–19 – ALIAKSANDR BUTRYM, andreiuc88. 20–21 – Dziurek, high fliers. 22–23 – Alexandre Laprise, e-leet. 24–25 – nasim. shikdar, GenadijsZ. 26–27 – Lysogor Roman, Vixit. 28–29 – Dmitry Molchanov, Marti Bug Catcher.

Bearport Publishing Company Product Development Team

President: Jen Jenson; Director of Product Development: Spencer Brinker; Managing Editor: Allison Juda; Associate Editor: Naomi Reich; Associate Editor: Tiana Tran; Art Director: Colin O'Dea; Designer: Elena Klinkner; Designer: Kayla Eggert; Product Development Assistant: Owen Hamlin

Library of Congress Cataloging-in-Publication Data is available at www.loc.gov or upon request from the publisher.

ISBN: 979-8-88916-594-1 (hardcover)
ISBN: 979-8-88916-599-6 (paperback)
ISBN: 979-8-88916-603-0 (ebook)

For more information, write to Bearport Publishing, 5357 Penn Avenue South, Minneapolis, MN 55419.

CONTENTS

THE BIG FREEZE

How would you feel if the whole world around you froze? What if it was covered in slippery ice?

If you don't like the cold, be warned . . .

IT'S AN ICE AGE!

What would you do if the whole world was covered in ice and snow?

It is time to become an ice age survival **expert.**

NOT THE FIRST NOR THE LAST

There have been five ice ages throughout history. And there are likely to be more.

The last ice age was 11,000 years ago. While some animals **adapted** to the cold, others died.

Woolly mammoths, saber-toothed cats, and cave bears went **extinct** as the weather changed again.

EXTINCT

Woolly mammoth

ABOVE AND BELOW

Watch out from above! During an ice age, ice might fall from the sky.

Hailstones can form in the clouds during freezing weather. They drop down as big balls of ice. Protect your head!

Hail is not the only frozen thing to look out for. There will be giant glaciers, too. These huge chunks of ice move like slow, frozen rivers.

Large blocks of ice could break off glaciers. If they fall into lakes or oceans, they may cause floods.

THE WARMEST PLACE ON EARTH

As the glaciers come closer, the weather will get colder. You will need to find somewhere warm.

Find your family and friends. It will be hard to see during **blizzards**. The more eyes, the better!

Head for the equator. This is near the middle of the planet.

The equator usually gets the most heat from the sun. That's your best bet to keep warm.

Once you reach the equator, it's time to settle down.

Choose the best spot for a **bunker**. Until the ice age ends, you will be here for a few years.

Grab a shovel and start digging.

EMERGENCY BACKUP PLAN

If you can't dig, try finding shelter somewhere else.

Step 1: Find a mountain.

Step 2: Look for a cave.

Step 3: Check to make sure it's safe.

Step 4: Gather some dry wood.

Step 5: Start a fire to keep warm.

PREPARE YOURSELF

You can't survive without tools.

Snowshoes stop you from sinking in the snow. Keep a shovel close by. You will need it to clear the way.

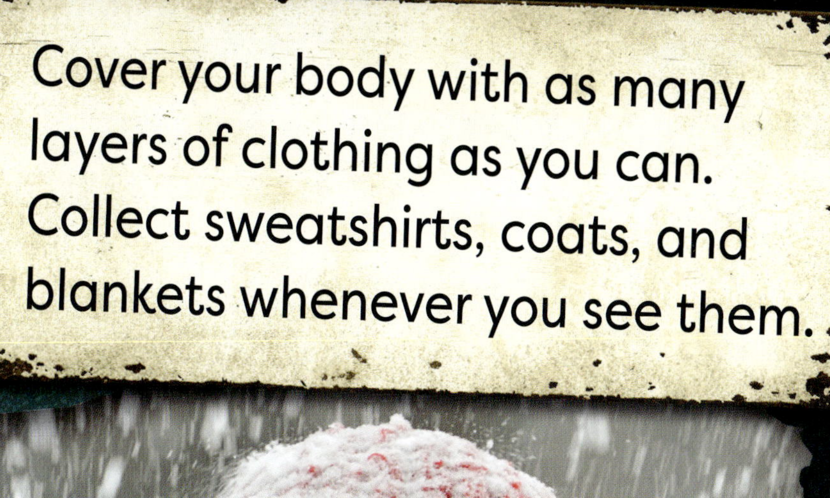

Cover your body with as many layers of clothing as you can. Collect sweatshirts, coats, and blankets whenever you see them.

The more layers you wear, the warmer you will be.

Another way to keep warm is by starting a fire.

Try finding dry pieces of wood. They burn more easily. If your fire gets out of control, use your shovel to dump snow on it.

A fire can also cook food and warm up drinks. **Stockpile** your shelter with plenty of food.

FINDING FOOD

Canned food will last the longest. But there are other ways of getting things to eat.

Learn about **foraging** outside. This is a way of looking for food in nature.

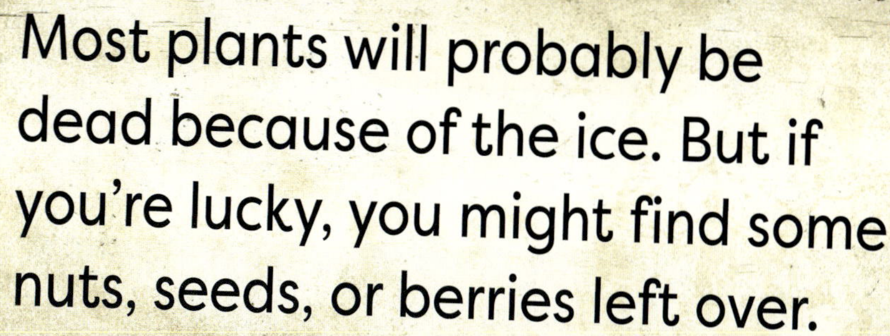

Most plants will probably be dead because of the ice. But if you're lucky, you might find some nuts, seeds, or berries left over.

WATCH OUT!

Stay with an adult when you go foraging. Some berries are **poisonous**.

If there are no berries and nuts, you may have to learn how to hunt.

With an adult, make a bow and arrow. Then, start hunting for some food.

Store any extra meat in ice. This keeps it fresh for your next meal.

Use bones to make tools, such as spears. Turn the fur into a warm coat.

As the years go by, the ice will start to melt. Rivers will begin to flow again, too.

The ice age is not over yet, but at least you can go fishing.

Perch on a rock to get a good view into the water.

Stand still and wait for fish. Once you spot one, quickly throw a spear into the water. Be careful not to fall in.

DISASTER AFTER DISASTER

As it heats up, more ice will melt. That may seem good. But all that water has to go somewhere.

As more ice melts, land will begin to flood. Towns and cities will soon be deep under water.

Switch out your snowshoes for a pair of rain boots. Find a boat to use on the water.

You can also head for higher ground. Find mountains or high hills to escape from the water.

Just know, mountains come with their own dangers. Melting snow and ice could break away from these tall landforms.

If this happens, giant chunks of ice may move very quickly down the sides of the mountain. This is called an avalanche (AV-uh-lanch).

Avalanches can cause serious harm. If you hear rumbling, quickly move to safety.

Keep your eyes open. A large white cloud of snow means an avalanche is just seconds away!

If an avalanche falls into the sea, you might be in for more trouble. This could cause giant waves.

These waves could wipe out everything in their path.

Stay on high ground. Look for other survivors.

Work together by teaching them everything you learned about being a survival expert.

THE DISASTER CHECKLIST

How should you brave the big freeze?

- ✓ Protect your head.
- ✓ Get with family and friends.
- ✓ Head to the equator.
- ✓ Find a place to stay.
- ✓ Make a fire.
- ✓ Gather supplies.
- ✓ Travel to higher ground.

GLOSSARY

adapted changed over time to survive in an environment

blizzards very heavy snowstorms with strong winds

bunker an underground shelter

expert someone who knows a lot about a subject

extinct when a type of animal completely dies out

foraging looking for food in the wild

poisonous dangerous or deadly when eaten

stockpile to save up a supply of something

INDEX

READ MORE

Collins, Ailynn. *Can You Survive the Schoolchildren's Blizzard? An Interactive History Adventure (You Choose: Disasters in History).* North Mankato, MN: Capstone Press, 2022.

Vonder Brink, Tracy. *Blizzards (Natural Disasters Where I Live).* Coral Springs, FL: Seahorse Publishing, 2022.

LEARN MORE ONLINE

1. Go to **www.factsurfer.com** or scan the QR code below.
2. Enter "**Braving Freeze**" into the search box.
3. Click on the cover of this book to see a list of websites.